Visiting History

by Rose Cully

Harcourt

SCHOOL PUBLISHERS

Cover and 3 Media Bakery, 4 Superstock, 5 Corbis, 6 Corbis, 7 Superstock, 8 Corbis, 9 Harcourt, 10 Corbis, 11 Media Bakery, 12 Shutterstock, 13 and 14 Media Bakery.

Printed in China

ISBN 10: 0-15-350319-X
ISBN 13: 978-0-15-350319-1

Ordering Options
ISBN 10: 0-15-349941-9 (Grade 6 ELL Collection)
ISBN 13: 978-0-15-349941-8 (Grade 6 ELL Collection)
ISBN 10: 0-15-357365-1 (package of 5)
ISBN 13: 978-0-15-357365-1 (package of 5)

5 6 7 8 9 10   0940   15 14 13 12 11 10 09

National Historic Landmarks

America's history is preserved, or kept alive, in many ways. Writing, photographs, songs, and films can each give us an idea of what life was like in other times. Places or objects can also help us know how life once was.

National Historic Landmarks are places or objects that are thought to be important to American history. They can be buildings, battle sites, ships, neighborhoods, and even a space vehicle. There are many historic places in the United States, but only about 2,500 have been named landmarks.

Washington Monument, Washington, D.C.

Who Chooses Landmarks?

The National Park Service is in charge of choosing these landmarks. The process often starts when citizens nominate a place or object to be a National Historic Landmark. Experts are needed to help in the process. An architect is needed if the place is a building. A historian, or someone who studies history, is needed if the place is a battle site. Then they decide which places are an important part of America's history and culture. The United States Secretary of the Interior makes the final choice.

It is an honor when a place is chosen to be a National Historic Landmark. The owner of the place gets a special sign with the landmark's name on it to put on the outside of the place. Then everyone can see that it is a National Historic Landmark.

Different Kinds of Landmarks

There are many different kinds of National Historic Landmarks in the United States. There are also a number of ways that visitors can see and enjoy the landmarks. People can walk through the neighborhood in Atlanta, Georgia, where Martin Luther King, Jr. lived. They can go to a concert in Carnegie Hall in New York. They can take a tour on a submarine, or they can stand where the first shots in the Revolutionary War rang out. They can even watch a car race at the Indianapolis Motor Speedway in Indiana!

Come along on a tour of some of our country's landmarks. Maybe one is near where you live!

Pictograph Cave *Billings, Montana*

Long ago, people used pictographs, or wall paintings, to record stories about their culture. During the 1930s, more than a hundred of them were found in one place. Archaeologists were excited to discover them in a cave in Billings, Montana. The Native Americans who made these pictures used just a few colors: white, black, and red. These pictures were made by artists who lived more than 1,500 years ago!

Taos Pueblo *Taos, New Mexico*

A pueblo is a kind of ancient apartment house. The word *pueblo* means "village" in Spanish. A whole village of Native Americans began living here—at the Taos Pueblo—more than 600 years ago! The pueblo is made of *adobe*, which is made from mud and straw. The mud and straw are mixed together and shaped into bricks. The bricks become hard when they are left in the sun to dry. The people in the village always worked together to raise crops. This was difficult because the area does not get much rain. Some relatives of the original builders of the pueblo continue to live there today.

Old South Meeting House *Boston, Massachusetts*

Town halls were very important in spreading news to people before television and radio. Town meetings were held so that people could get information and make any announcements they might have had. The Old South Meeting House was the type of place where this happened.

On December 16, 1773, 5,000 colonists met at the Old South Meeting House to protest a tax on tea. That was when the Sons of Liberty planned the Boston Tea Party. That was one of the events that led up to the Revolutionary War.

United States Capitol *Washington, D.C.*

The United States Capitol is where our Congress meets to decide on America's laws. It is also one of our country's most well-known buildings. The building was begun in 1793, when George Washington was the President of the United States.

Independence Rock *Casper, Wyoming*

In the 1800s, the trip west was a very long one. People traveling along the Oregon Trail rested at Independence Rock in Casper, Wyoming. Many travelers painted the names of their family members on the rock while they were there. Others would use a sharp object to carve their names into the rock. Those names are still there! Today Independence Rock reminds visitors of the people who made the difficult journey west.

Brooklyn Bridge *New York, New York*

Every day, thousands of people use the Brooklyn Bridge to drive between Manhattan and Brooklyn in New York City. Many others walk across the bridge along a sidewalk made just for pedestrians.

The building of this huge structure began almost 150 years ago, long before cars. Architect John Roebling designed the bridge but died soon after construction started in 1869. His son, Washington A. Roebling, made sure that the bridge was finished. This bridge was the very first to use stainless steel cables. This bridge was also the largest suspension bridge in the world at the time it was finished.

11

Rose Bowl Stadium *Pasadena, California*

Some people think that the Rose Bowl is the most important game in college football. Every year the game is played on or around New Year's Day. The Rose Bowl has been held almost every year since 1923 in the same place—the Rose Bowl Stadium. These days it holds more than 90,000 people! That's a lot of people in one place!

Empire State Building *New York, New York*

The Empire State Building was built in less than 14 months. It was the world's tallest building when it was finished in 1931. You would have to walk four city blocks—over one-fourth of a mile (0.44 km)—to cover the distance from the bottom of the Empire State Building to the top. An elevator in the building takes you up to an observation deck at the top. It is no longer the world's tallest building. Still, the view of New York City from the top is amazing. The busy people and noisy cars on the streets below look like ants!

Empire State Building

Gateway Arch *St. Louis, Missouri*

The Gateway Arch in St. Louis, Missouri, is one of the largest monuments in the United States. This 630-foot-high (192 m) structure made of shiny stainless steel was built in 1963. It was designed by Eero Saarinen, a famous architect from the country of Finland.

It was built to remember the Louisiana Purchase. In 1803, the United States bought a huge piece of land from France. This land makes up a large part of the United States today. The Gateway Arch is a symbol of the gate to the West. You may want to enjoy the exciting tram ride to the top before heading West!

There are National Historic Landmarks all over the United States. Perhaps there's one in your neighborhood you can visit!

Scaffolded Language Development

USING PASSIVE VOICE When a sentence is written in the passive voice, the subject of the sentence receives the action. For example: *The Empire State Building was built in less than 14 months.* Point out that in this sentence, the Empire State Building is the subject that was being built. Sentences in the passive voice include a form of the verb *to be*. Point out the word *was* in the sentence. Suggest that instead of using the passive voice, using the active voice makes writing more interesting. For example: *It took less than 14 months to build the Empire State Building.*

Help students rewrite the following sentences, transforming them from active to passive voice. Ask volunteers to read their answers aloud.

1. Thousands of years ago, people drew pictures on cave walls.
2. Someone gave the Statue of Liberty to the United States as a gift.
3. People used cables to build the Brooklyn Bridge.
4. In 1729, someone constructed the Old South Meeting House.
5. People can hear concerts at Carnegie Hall.

Social Studies

Where Is It? Provide a copy of an outline map of the United States for students. Help students find the locations of the National Historic Landmarks in the book on a classroom map of the United States. Then have them mark and label their own map with the location of each landmark.

School-Home Connection
National Historic Landmarks Have students share with family members information about some of the National Historic Landmarks in the book. Have them discuss places in their own community that might be on the list of landmarks.

Word Count: 1,169